Usborne
1000
THINGS IN
NATURE

Illustrated by Mar Ferrero

Edited by Hannah Watson
Designed by Yasmin Faulkner

Expert advice from Dr John Rostron
and Dr Margaret Rostron

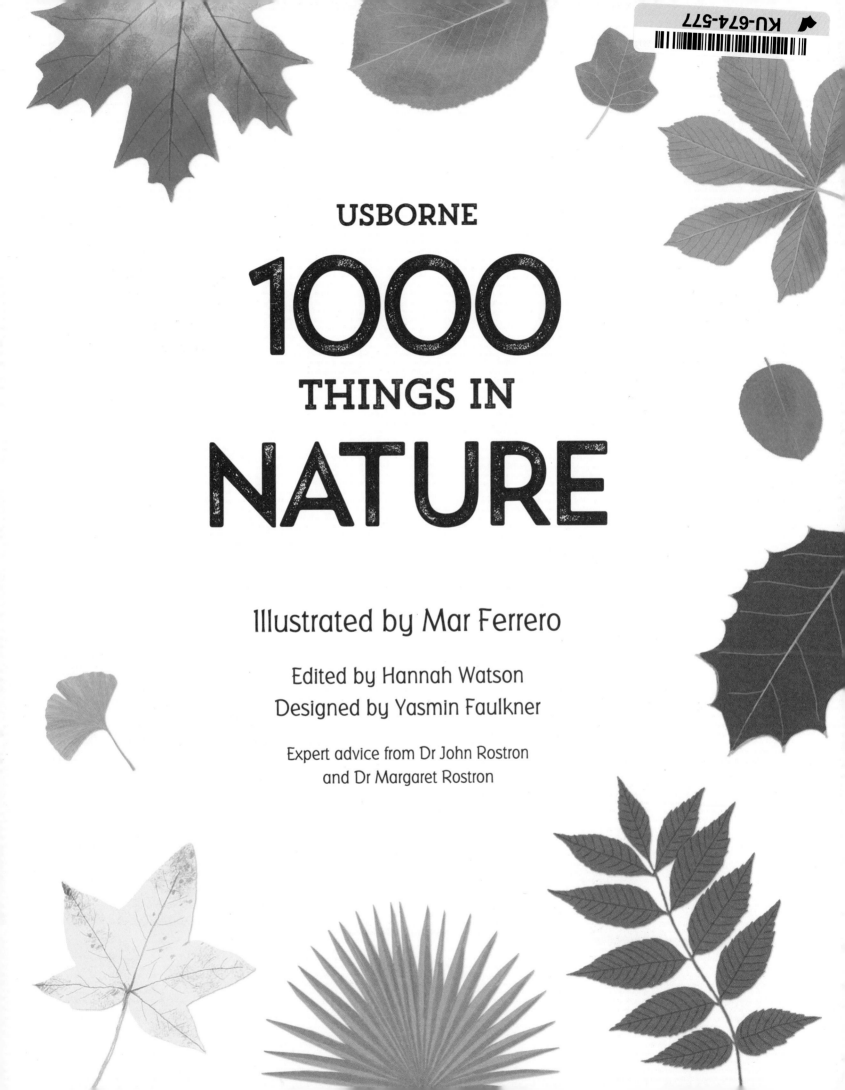

Contents

Meadows and hedgerows
Page 5

In a garden
Page 6

Feathers, eggs and nests
Page 7

Creepy-crawlies
Page 8

Fruits, leaves and seeds
Page 9

Plants and flowers
Page 10

In the jungle
Pages 11-12

Woodlands and forests
Pages 13-14

In the mountains
Page 15

Savannahs and grasslands
Page 16

In the desert
Page 17

Ice and snow
Page 18

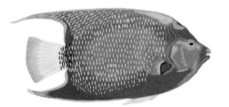

Under the sea
Pages 19-20

Ponds and lakes
Page 21

Streams and rivers
Page 22

By the coast
Page 23

Farms and fields
Page 24

Food from nature
Pages 25-26

Lots of trees
Pages 27-28

Fossils, rocks and gems
Page 29

Meadows and hedgerows

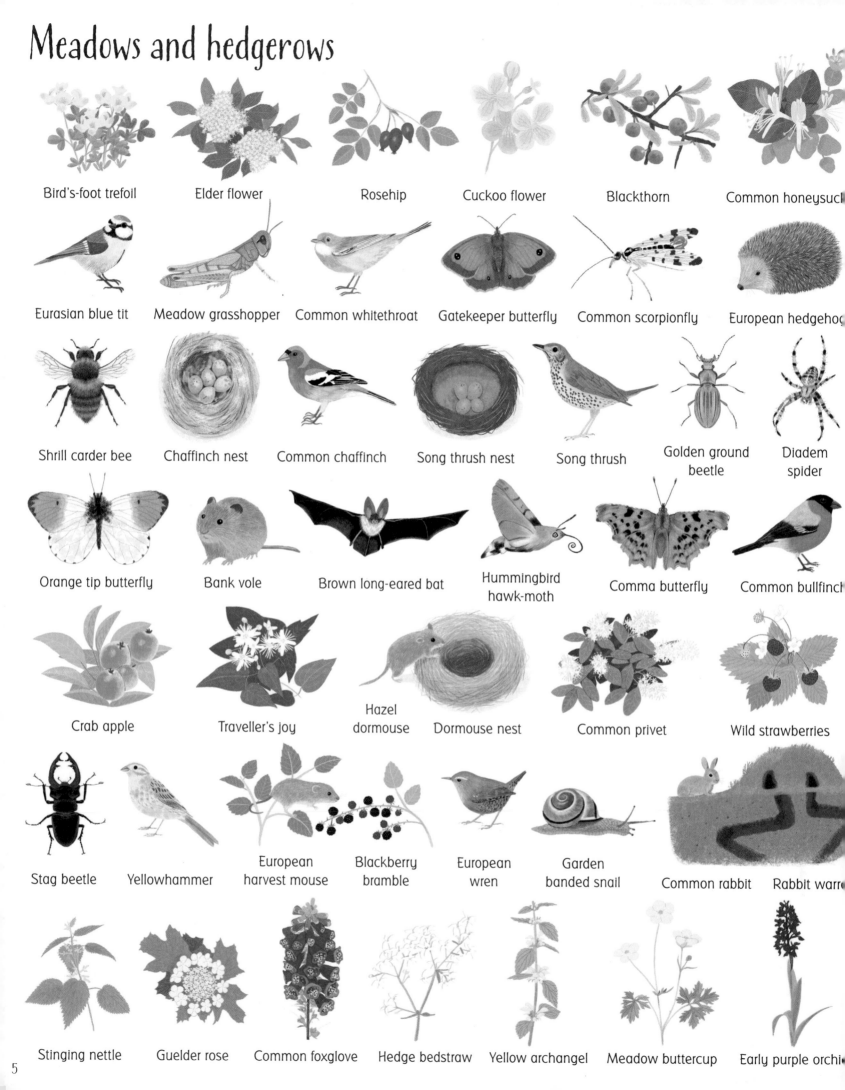

Bird's-foot trefoil

Elder flower

Rosehip

Cuckoo flower

Blackthorn

Common honeysuckle

Eurasian blue tit

Meadow grasshopper

Common whitethroat

Gatekeeper butterfly

Common scorpionfly

European hedgehog

Shrill carder bee

Chaffinch nest

Common chaffinch

Song thrush nest

Song thrush

Golden ground beetle

Diadem spider

Orange tip butterfly

Bank vole

Brown long-eared bat

Hummingbird hawk-moth

Comma butterfly

Common bullfinch

Crab apple

Traveller's joy

Hazel dormouse

Dormouse nest

Common privet

Wild strawberries

Stag beetle

Yellowhammer

European harvest mouse

Blackberry bramble

European wren

Garden banded snail

Common rabbit

Rabbit warren

Stinging nettle

Guelder rose

Common foxglove

Hedge bedstraw

Yellow archangel

Meadow buttercup

Early purple orchid

n a garden

House sparrow

Dark-eyed junco

Common starling

European greenfinch

American robin

European robin

Tawny owl

Common wasp

Peacock butterfly

Stone centipede

Speckled bush-cricket

Black garden ant

Common woodlouse

European mole

House mouse

European honeybee

Snail shell

Garden snail

Housefly

Domestic cat

Red fox

North American raccoon

Grey squirrel

Common frog

Wood mouse

ughing kookaburra

Garden bumblebee

Seven-spot ladybird

Common wood pigeon

Red Admiral butterfly

European badger

Common shrew

Long-tailed tit

Holly blue butterfly

Noisy miner

Flowering cherry

Leyland cypress

Pipistrelle bat

Brown rat

Common earthworm

Black slug

Common ivy

White clover

Tall fescue grass

Common laburnum

Common dandelion

Common daisy

Feathers, eggs and nests

Mandarin
duck feather

Great spotted
woodpecker feather

Peacock feather

King bird-of-
paradise feather

Ostrich
feather

European jay
feather

Mute swan
feather

Alexandrine
parakeet feat

Pheasant
feather

Blue-fronted
Amazon feather

Red-crested
turaco feather

Flamingo
feather

Golden oriole
feather

Golden-headed
quetzal feather

Chukar
partridge feather

Mallard
feather

Screech o
feather

Ostrich egg

Emu egg

Southern cassowary egg

Common
murre egg

Golden
eagle egg

Maran
chicken egg

European
buzzard eg

Elegant crested
tinamou egg

Guira
cuckoo egg

Eurasian
sparrowhawk egg

Mistle
thrush egg

American
robin egg

Red-winged
blackbird egg

Common reed
bunting egg

Dunnock
egg

House
wren e

Anna's
hummingbird nest

Lappet-faced
vulture nest

Cetti's warbler nest

Bald eagle nest

Eurasian coot nest

Little grebe nest

Harris hawk nest

Ovenbird nest

Sociable
weaver nests

American cliff
swallow nest

Montezuma
oropendola nest

Baya weaver
nest

Eurasian
penduline tit nes

7

Creepy-crawlies

een tiger beetle

Eastern lubber grasshopper

Colorado beetle

Picasso bug

Daring jumping spider

Mexican red-kneed tarantula

Grass cross spider

mblebee millipede

Florida blue centipede

Eastern striped cricket

Mosquito

Spotted cranefly

American cockroach

Blue morpho utterfly's eggs

Blue morpho butterfly

Monarch caterpillar

Monarch butterfly

Monarch butterfly's chrysalis

Burnet moth's cocoon

Bald-faced hornet's nest

Bald-faced hornet

Oak marble galls

Oak marble gall wasp

Potter wasp's nests

Yellow potter wasp

Paper wasp's nest

European paper wasp

Cinnabar caterpillar

Cinnabar moth

Forest tent caterpillar

Forest tent caterpillar moth

Spotted oleander caterpillar

Spotted oleander caterpillar moth

Green shield bug's eggs

Green shield bug

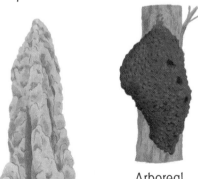
Cathedral termite mound

Arboreal termite nest

Cathedral termite

Magnetic termite mound

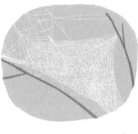
Money spider's web

Funnel-web spider's web

Orbweaver spider's web

Green lacewing's eggs

Praying mantis

Spittlebug foam

Two-lined spittlebug

Green lacewing

Fruits, leaves and seeds

Sugar maple leaf

Cabbage palmetto leaf

Common pear leaf

Maidenhair tree leaf

English oak leaf

Rowan leaf

Horse chestnut leaf

Cycad cone

Acorn

Atlas cedar cone

Conker

Norway spruce cone

Ohio buckeye seed

Aleppo pine cone

Apple pips   Apple

Avocado   Avocado stone

Cherry   Cherry stone

Peach   Peach stone

Pumpkin seeds

Sunflower seeds

Leaf buds

Sweetgum leaf

Holly leaf

Tulip tree leaf

Common sundew leaf

Mustard seeds

Sesame seeds

Atlas cedar leaves

Common ash leaf

Dawn redwood leaves

Zebra plant leaf

Norfolk Island pine leaves

Crack willow leaf

Leaf skeleton

Norway spruce leaves

Field maple seeds

White ash seed

Eastern redbud seed pod

Burdock burrs

Milkweed seed pod

Great hairy willowherb seed pod

Dandelion clock

Plants and flowers

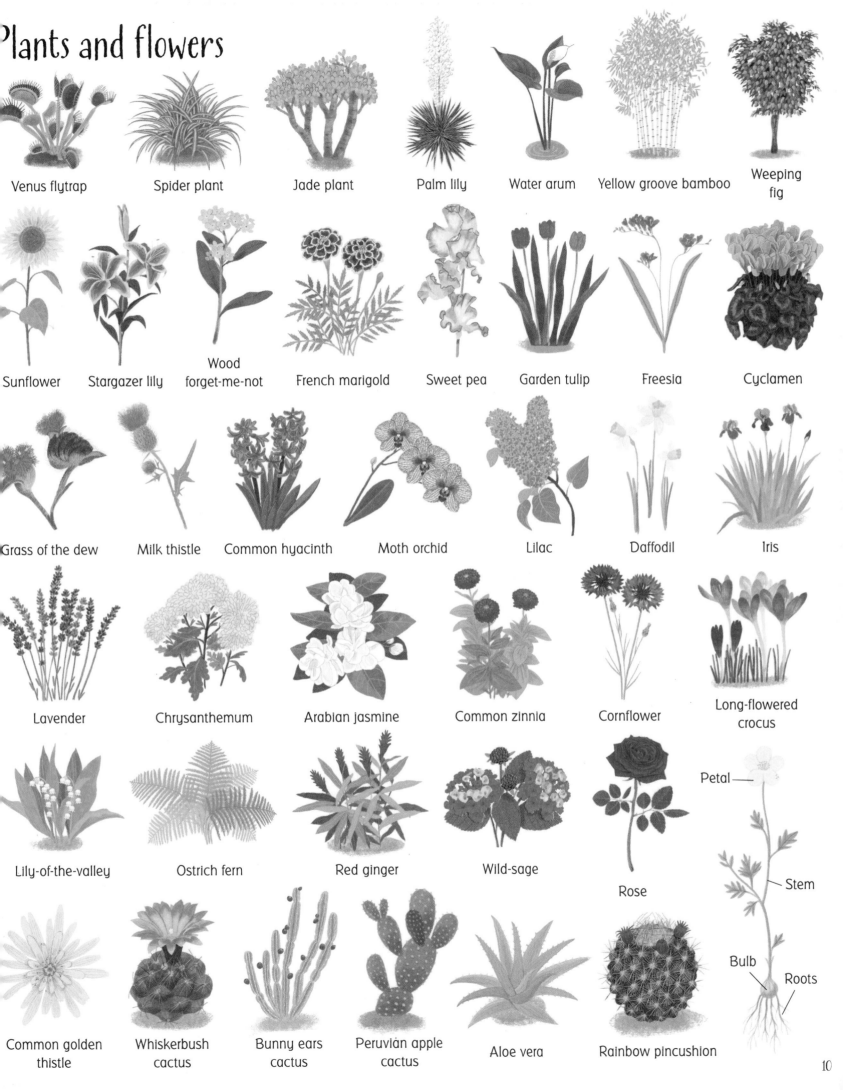

Venus flytrap

Spider plant

Jade plant

Palm lily

Water arum

Yellow groove bamboo

Weeping fig

Sunflower

Stargazer lily

Wood forget-me-not

French marigold

Sweet pea

Garden tulip

Freesia

Cyclamen

Grass of the dew

Milk thistle

Common hyacinth

Moth orchid

Lilac

Daffodil

Iris

Lavender

Chrysanthemum

Arabian jasmine

Common zinnia

Cornflower

Long-flowered crocus

Lily-of-the-valley

Ostrich fern

Red ginger

Wild-sage

Rose

Petal

Stem

Bulb

Roots

Common golden thistle

Whiskerbush cactus

Bunny ears cactus

Peruvian apple cactus

Aloe vera

Rainbow pincushion

In the jungle

Black-and-yellow broadbill

Moustached babbler

Wilson's bird-of-paradise

Mealy Amazon

Crimson-breasted flowerpecker

Black-capped lory

Blue-and-yellow macaw

Rainbow stag beetle

Army ant

Goliath bird-eater spider

Hercules beetle

Madagascar giraffe weevil

Lesser anteater

Central America agouti

False bird-of-paradise

Passion fruit flower

Stingless Mayan bee

Peacock flower

Victoria waterlily

Rafflesia

Queen Alexandra birdwing butterfly

Bengal tiger

Black-and-white ruffed lemur

Jaguar

Mandrill

Ocelot

Sumatran orangutan

Malay fruit bat

Brown-throated sloth

Okapi

Bongo

Orangutan nest

Red mangrove

Walking palm

Brazil nut tree

Red cecropia

Kapok tree

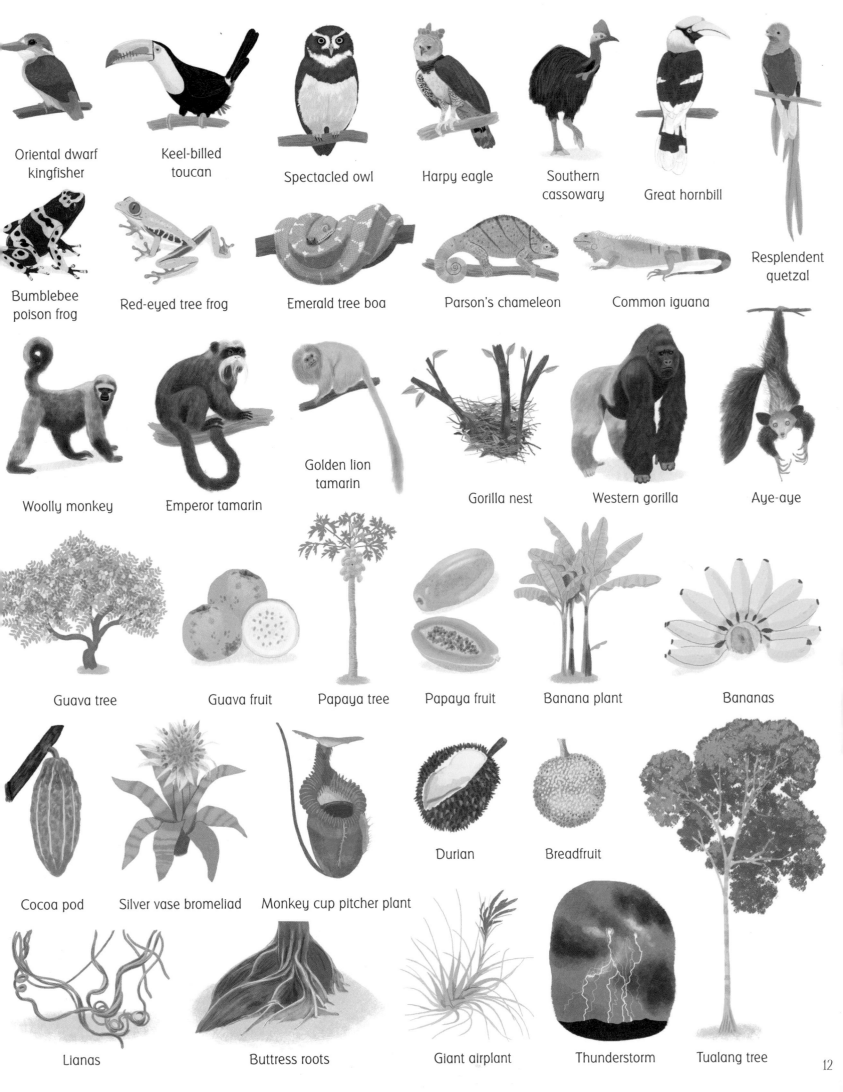

Oriental dwarf kingfisher

Keel-billed toucan

Spectacled owl

Harpy eagle

Southern cassowary

Great hornbill

Resplendent quetzal

Bumblebee poison frog

Red-eyed tree frog

Emerald tree boa

Parson's chameleon

Common iguana

Woolly monkey

Emperor tamarin

Golden lion tamarin

Gorilla nest

Western gorilla

Aye-aye

Guava tree

Guava fruit

Papaya tree

Papaya fruit

Banana plant

Bananas

Cocoa pod

Silver vase bromeliad

Monkey cup pitcher plant

Durian

Breadfruit

Lianas

Buttress roots

Giant airplant

Thunderstorm

Tualang tree

12

Woodlands and forests

Cloudberry

Canadian bunchberry

Sanicle

Bell heather

Bilberry

Bracken

Black morel mushroom

Long-eared owl

Owl pellet

Fly agaric mushroom

Lewis's woodpecker

Fishbone beard lichen

Canada lynx

Penny bun mushroom

Spotted owl

Sharp-shinned hawk

American black bear

North American porcupine

Gopher tortoise

European pine marten

Eurasian wolf

Western swordfern

Larch silkworm

Squirrel's drey

American red squirrel

Pine mushroom

Red crossbill

Juniper webworm

Grizzly bear

Canadian hemlock

Atlas cedar

Queensland kauri pine

Douglas fir

Yew plum pine

Golden jelly fungus

Turkey tail mushroom

Indigo milk cap mushroom

Frost's bolete mushroom

Devil's matchstick lichen

Common greenshield lichen

Cinnabar chanterelle

Fallow deer

White-tailed deer

Shed deer antler

Timber rattlesnake

Common toad

Spotted salamander

English holly

Lesser celandine

Enchanter's nightshade

Hop hornbeam catkin

Greater butterfly orchid

Common bluebell

Southern arrowwood

Eastern chipmunk

Striped skunk

Virginia opossum

Little brown bat

Wild boar

picebush swallowtail

Spotted longhorn beetle

Poplar hawk-moth

Ruffed grouse

Northern cardinal

Blue jay

Blue jay nest

Common beech

Dawn redwood

Silver birch

English oak

Pileated woodpecker

In the mountains

Purple-edged copper butterfly

Phoebus Apollo butterfly

Mountain fritillary butterfly

Alpine swift

Golden eagle

Andean condor

Mountain qu

White asphodel

Bearded bellflower

Silky phacelia

Starry saxifrage

Mountain everlasting

Flower of the Andes

Alpenrose

Alpine snowbe

Snow leopard

Cougar

Alpine ibex

Fjord horse

Rocky Mountain goat

Rocky Mountain elk

Himalaya brown bea

Pixie cup lichen

New Zealand cushion plant

Glory-of-the-snow

Mountain cornflower

Iceland moss

Alpine rock-jasmine

Dwarf willow

Alpine marmot

Marmot burrow

Golden alpine salamander

Alpine newt

Alpine bullhead

Sunapee golden trout

Brook trout

Quaking aspen

Common juniper

Silver spruce

Mountain hemlock

Queen of the Andes

Rock pinnacle

Greenschist

Argillite

Rocky outcro

avannahs and grasslands

Kopje

Umbrella thorn acacia

Jackalberry tree

Monkey-bread tree

Candelabra tree

Lilac-breasted roller

Budgerigar

Red-billed hornbill

Short-eared owl

Blue-winged parrotlet

Turquoise-browed motmot

Common kestrel

Plains zebra

African buffalo

Blue wildebeest

American bison

Common warthog

Impala

Gerenuk

Southern white rhinoceros

Southern brown bandicoot

Nine-banded armadillo

Ground pangolin

Hamadryas baboon

Animal dung

Dung beetle

Bat-eared fox

Spotted hyena

West African lion

Black-tailed prairie dog

Serval

South African cheetah

Boomslang snake

African rock python

Saddle-billed stork

Vulturine guineafowl

Common ostrich

Masai giraffe

Buffalo grass

Big bluestem grass

Kangaroo grass

Pampas grass

African foxtail grass

Waterhole

In the desert

Sahara desert ant

Camel spider

Giant hairy scorpion

Arizona coral snake

Arizona blond tarantula

Gila monster

Thorny dragon

Meerkat

Namibian desert elephant

Red kangaroo

Ladder-backed woodpecker

Elf owl

Gambel's quail

Gilded flicker

Teddy-bear cholla

Big galleta

Fishhook barrel cactus

Desert sunflower

Beavertail cactus

Jojoba fruit

Broad-billed hummingbird

Ocotillo flower

Oasis

Animal bones

Shed snake skin

Tumbleweed

Sand dune

Sandstorm

Aardwolf

Indian desert jird

Sand cat

Sidewinder

Antelope jackrabbit

Dromedary

Fennec fo

Desert fan palm

Desert willow

Joshua tree

Saguaro cactus

Camel thorn

Desert pavement

Uluru / Ayers Rock

Canyon

Fairy chimney

Dust dev

ce and snow

Arctic fox

Siberian tiger

Polar bear

Arctic hare

Alaskan moose

Svalbard reindeer

Antarctic pearlwort

White cottongrass

Common bearberry

Arctic woolly bear caterpillar

Arctic woolly bear moth

Norway lemming

Ermine

Emperor penguin

Adélie penguin

Snowy owl

Rough-legged buzzard

Northern fulmar

Snow petrel

Wandering albatross

Rock ptarmigan

Narwhal

Atlantic walrus

Bearded seal

Mackerel icefish

Humpback whale

Beluga whale

Arctic char

Patagonian toothfish

Bowhead whale

Antarctic krill

Snowflakes

Reindeer lichen

Watermelon snow

Soft rime

Needle ice

Penitentes snow formation

Snow chimney

Icicles

Glacier

Avalanche

Iceberg

Glacier cave

Ice floe

Frozen waterfall

Under the sea

Red sea fan

Magnificent sea anemone

Bubblegum coral

Sea apple

Pacific strawberry anemone

Stove-pipe sponge

Carnation coral

Great white shark

Whale shark

Great hammerhead shark

Basking shark

Pillow lava

Manganese nodule

Blue whale

Sperm whale

Zebra seahorse

Lined seahorse

Dwarf seahorse

Black-lip pearl oyster

Seamount

Submarine volcano

Hydrothermal vent

Bubble snail

Orange clownfish

Forceps butterflyfish

Royal angelfish

Flagtail surgeonfish

Queen angelfish

Coral reef

Finless porpoise

Common bottlenose dolphin

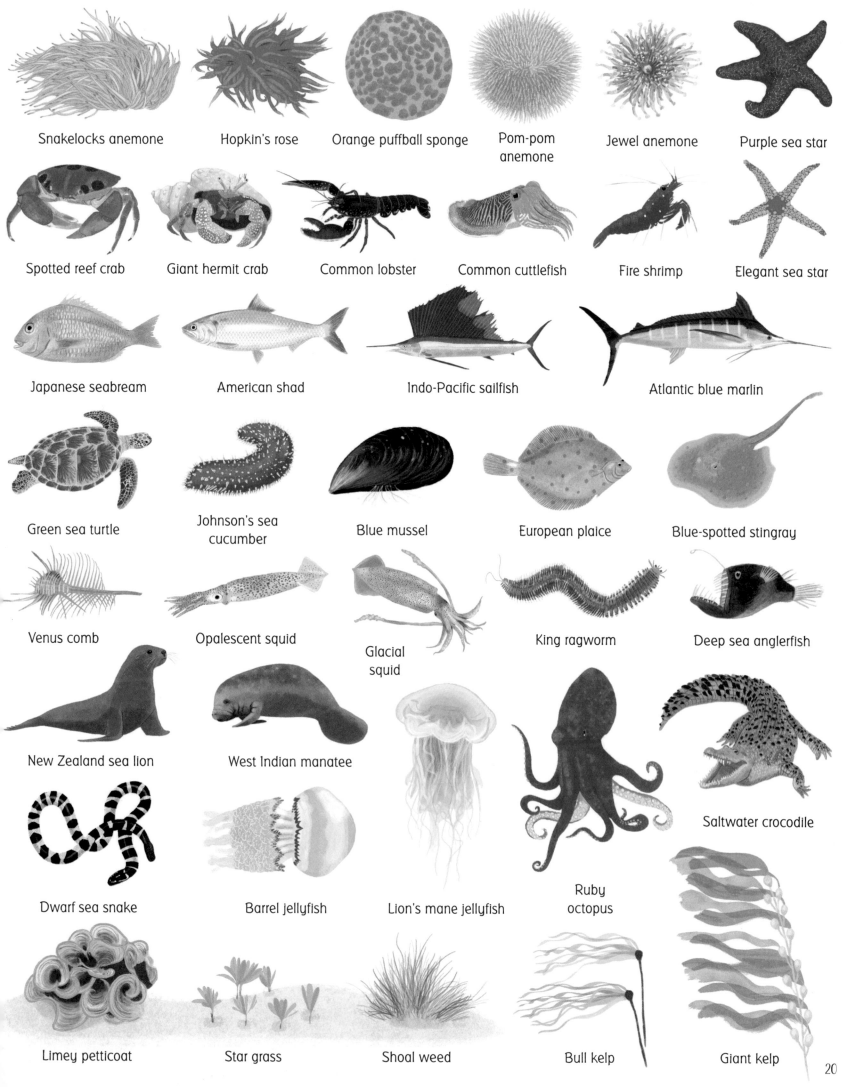

Snakelocks anemone

Hopkin's rose

Orange puffball sponge

Pom-pom anemone

Jewel anemone

Purple sea star

Spotted reef crab

Giant hermit crab

Common lobster

Common cuttlefish

Fire shrimp

Elegant sea star

Japanese seabream

American shad

Indo-Pacific sailfish

Atlantic blue marlin

Green sea turtle

Johnson's sea cucumber

Blue mussel

European plaice

Blue-spotted stingray

Venus comb

Opalescent squid

Glacial squid

King ragworm

Deep sea anglerfish

New Zealand sea lion

West Indian manatee

Saltwater crocodile

Dwarf sea snake

Barrel jellyfish

Lion's mane jellyfish

Ruby octopus

Limey petticoat

Star grass

Shoal weed

Bull kelp

Giant kelp

Ponds and lakes

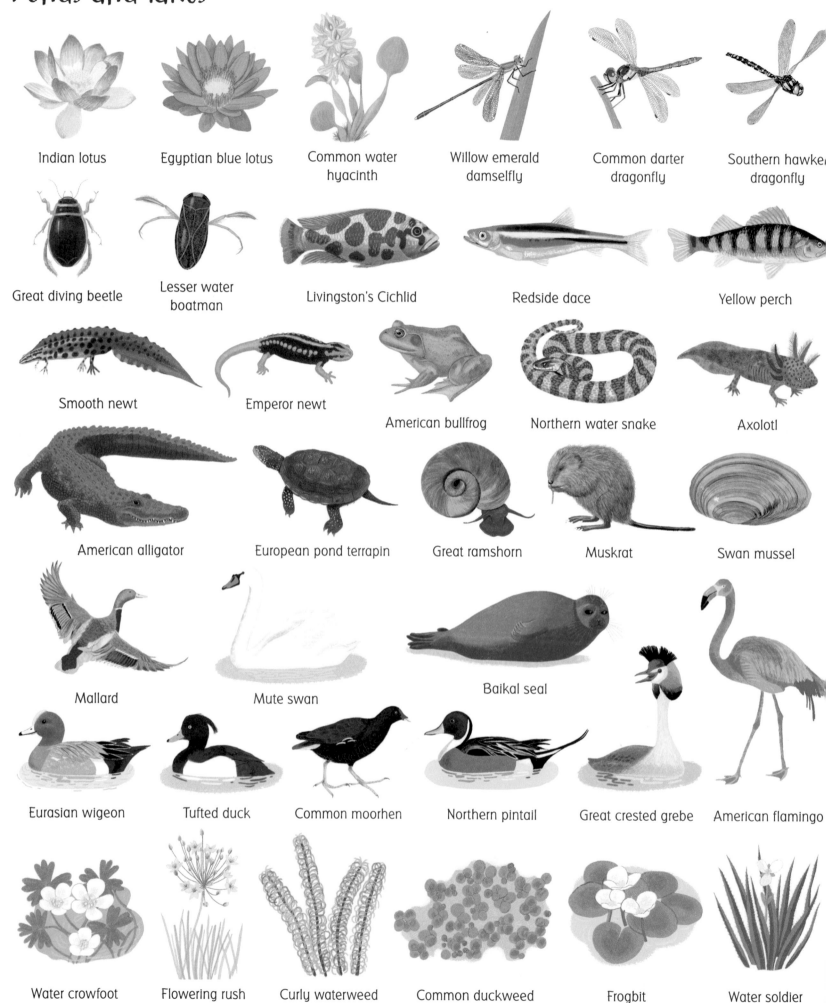

Indian lotus

Egyptian blue lotus

Common water hyacinth

Willow emerald damselfly

Common darter dragonfly

Southern hawker dragonfly

Great diving beetle

Lesser water boatman

Livingston's Cichlid

Redside dace

Yellow perch

Smooth newt

Emperor newt

American bullfrog

Northern water snake

Axolotl

American alligator

European pond terrapin

Great ramshorn

Muskrat

Swan mussel

Mallard

Mute swan

Baikal seal

Eurasian wigeon

Tufted duck

Common moorhen

Northern pintail

Great crested grebe

American flamingo

Water crowfoot

Flowering rush

Curly waterweed

Common duckweed

Frogbit

Water soldier

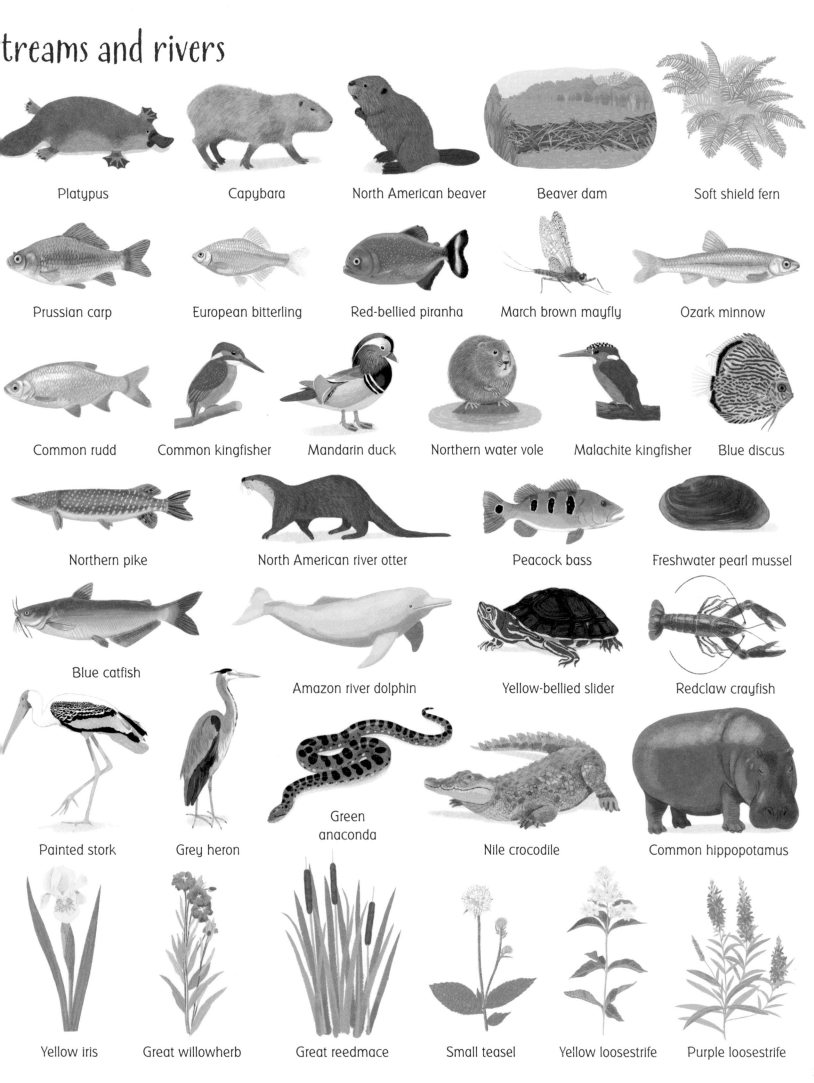

treams and rivers

Platypus

Capybara

North American beaver

Beaver dam

Soft shield fern

Prussian carp

European bitterling

Red-bellied piranha

March brown mayfly

Ozark minnow

Common rudd

Common kingfisher

Mandarin duck

Northern water vole

Malachite kingfisher

Blue discus

Northern pike

North American river otter

Peacock bass

Freshwater pearl mussel

Blue catfish

Amazon river dolphin

Yellow-bellied slider

Redclaw crayfish

Painted stork

Grey heron

Green
anaconda

Nile crocodile

Common hippopotamus

Yellow iris

Great willowherb

Great reedmace

Small teasel

Yellow loosestrife

Purple loosestrife

By the coast

Queen conch shell

Scallop shell

Netted dog whelk shell

Atlantic puffin

Common shelduck

European herring gull

Great white pelico

Orange sea lichen

Beadlet anemone

Sand dollar

Common limpet

Common sea urchin

European painted top shell

Sand

Driftwood

Fossil shark's tooth

Shark egg case

Knobbed whelk egg case

Moon snail egg collar

Sea turtle nest

Cuttlebo

Harbour porpoise

Northern minke whale

Short-beaked common dolphin

Mediterranean monk se

Sea pink

Sea kale

Sea lettuce

Knotted wrack

Florida pompano

Yellowfin goatfish

Coconut

Coconut palm

Sea stack

Leatherback sea turtle

Yellow seahorse

Yellow horned poppy

Golden samph

Beach cliff

Sea cave

Natural arch

Shingle

Farms and fields

Soya beans

Rapeseed

Barley

Rye

Flax

Sorghum

Rice plant

Common wheat

Cassava

Pumpkin

Cotton

Sugar beet

Maize

Potatoes

Embden goose

Common pheasant

Helmeted guineafowl

Grey partridge

Bourbon red turkey

Abacot ranger duck

Barn owl

Provence donkey

Provence foal

Merino lamb

Merino sheep

Scottish blackface sheep

Border collie

German shepherd

Boer goat

Angora goat

Angora kid

Jersey calf

Jersey cow

Friesian cow

Striped field mouse

Orpington hen

Orpington chick

Sussex cock

Hampshire pig

British Landrace piglet

British Landrace pig

European hare

Poitou donkey

Shire horse

Shire foal

Highland pony

Appaloosa mule

24

Food from nature

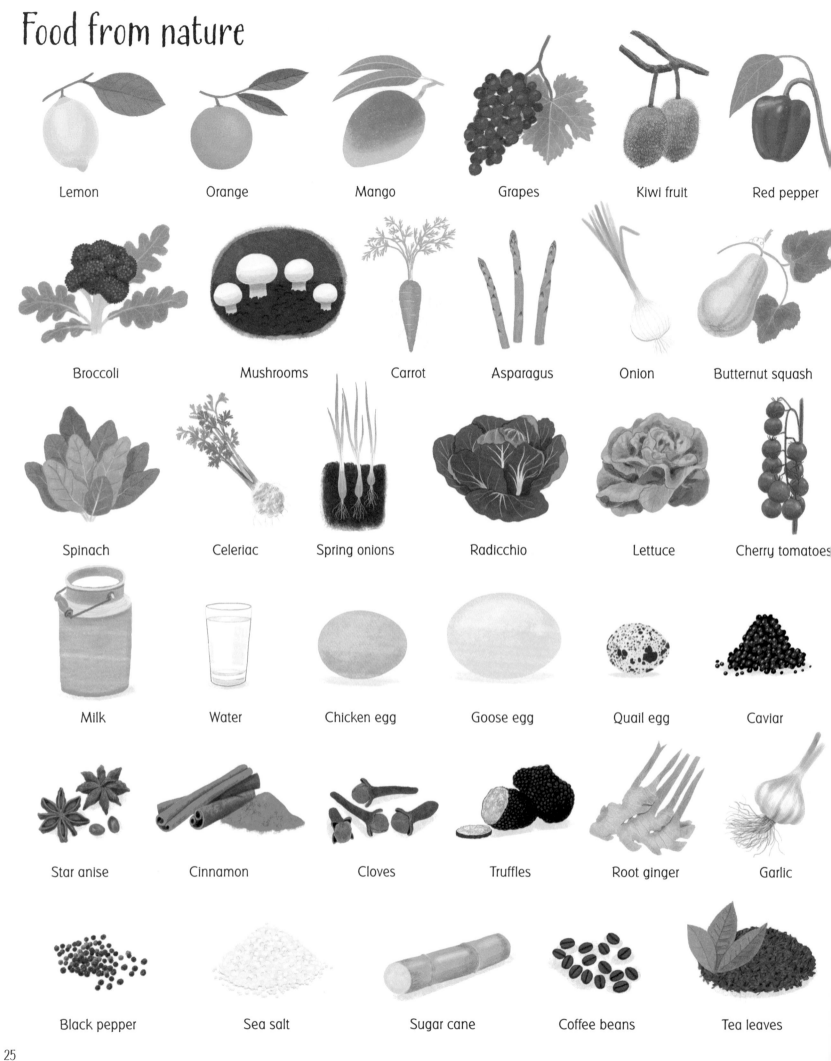

Lemon

Orange

Mango

Grapes

Kiwi fruit

Red pepper

Broccoli

Mushrooms

Carrot

Asparagus

Onion

Butternut squash

Spinach

Celeriac

Spring onions

Radicchio

Lettuce

Cherry tomatoes

Milk

Water

Chicken egg

Goose egg

Quail egg

Caviar

Star anise

Cinnamon

Cloves

Truffles

Root ginger

Garlic

Black pepper

Sea salt

Sugar cane

Coffee beans

Tea leaves

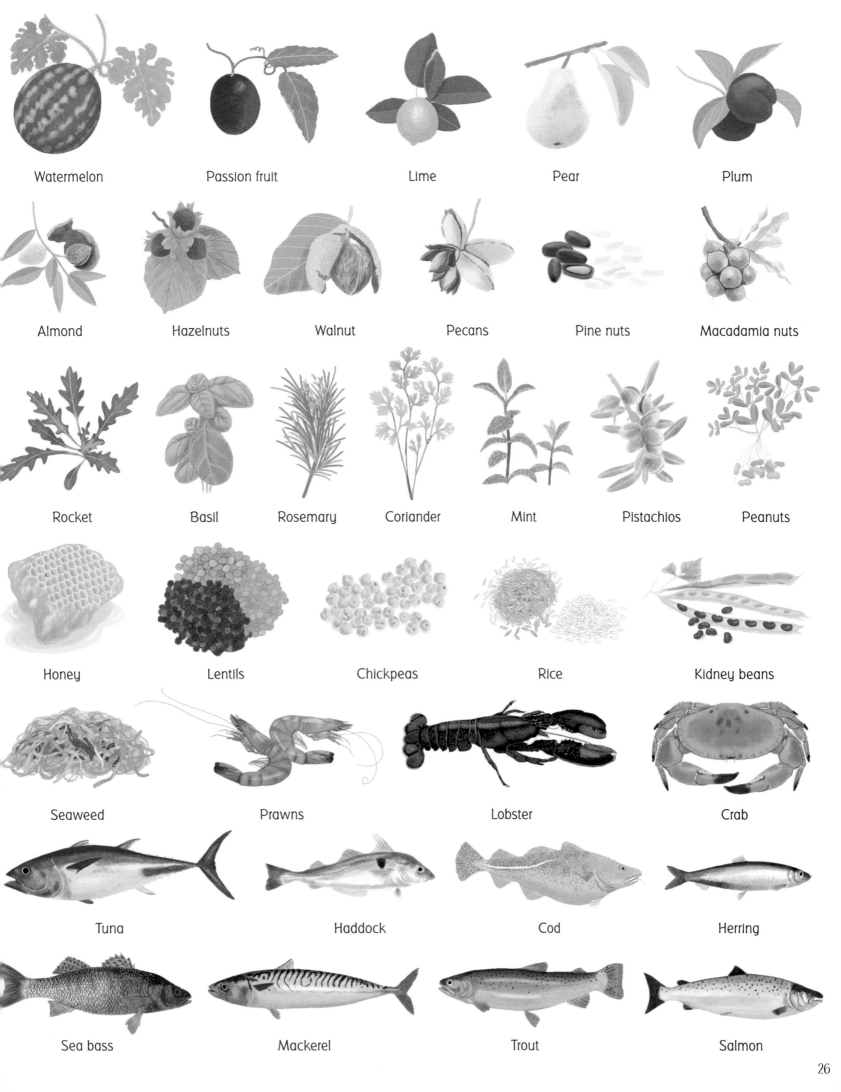

Watermelon

Passion fruit

Lime

Pear

Plum

Almond

Hazelnuts

Walnut

Pecans

Pine nuts

Macadamia nuts

Rocket

Basil

Rosemary

Coriander

Mint

Pistachios

Peanuts

Honey

Lentils

Chickpeas

Rice

Kidney beans

Seaweed

Prawns

Lobster

Crab

Tuna

Haddock

Cod

Herring

Sea bass

Mackerel

Trout

Salmon

Lots of trees

African mulberry

Sweet orange tree

Common hawthorn

Russian larch

Japanese cherry

Scots pine

Canada red chokecherry

European ash

Grandidier's baobab

English yew

Silver tree

Sycamore tree

Bay tree

Black poplar

Pignut hickory

Deodar cedar

Toddy palm

Mediterranean cypress

London plane

Giant quiver tree

Umbrella tree

American elm

European beech

Horse chestnut tree

Honey locust

Silver fir

Dragon blood tree

Scarlet oak

Rowan tree

Blue jacaranda

Giant redwood

Maidenhair tree

Tree aloe

Weeping
golden willow

Fig tree

Black cherry plum

Mount Etna broom

Great Basin
Bristlecone pine

Monkey puzzle
tree

Apple tree

Australian baobab

Northern red oak

Utah juniper

Wollemi pine

Pear tree

Mountain
cabbage tree

King palm

Western hemlock

Real fan palm

Boojum tree

Snowy mespilus

Kokerboom

Flamboyant tree

Olive tree

Teak

Common walnut tree

Sugar maple

Stone pine bark

Chinese paperbark
maple bark

Rainbow
eucalyptus bark

Paper birch bark

28

Fossils, rocks and gems

Red jasper

Garnet

Red beryl

Rhodonite

Agate

Topaz

Limestone

Granite

Fool's gold

Gold

Garnierite

Serpentine

Peridot

Emerald

Jade

Turquoise

Aquamarine

Alexandrite

Opal

Sapphire

Lapis lazuli

Thunderegg

Amethyst

Geode

Tourmaline

Rose quartz

Seed fern fossil

Fossil wood

Diamond

Marble

Silver

Stalagmite

Stalactite

Slate

Chalk

Coal

Pumice

Sandstone

Sea star fossil

Ammonite fossil

Trilobite fossil

Echinoid fossil

Flint

Belemnite fos

Index

A

Aardwolf 17
Abacot ranger duck 24
Acorn 9
Adélie penguin 18
African buffalo 16
African foxtail grass 16
African mulberry 27
African rock python 16
Agate 29
Alaskan moose 18
Aleppo pine cone 9
Alexandrine parakeet feather 7
Alexandrite 29
Alligator, American 21
Almond 26
Aloe vera 10
Alpenrose 15
Alpine bullhead 15
Alpine ibex 15
Alpine marmot 15
Alpine newt 15
Alpine rock-jasmine 15
Alpine snowbell 15
Alpine swift 15
Amazon river dolphin 22
American alligator 21
American bison 16
American black bear 13
American bullfrog 21
American cliff swallow nest 7
American cockroach 8
American elm 27
American flamingo 21
American red squirrel 13
American robin 6
American robin egg 7
American shad 20
Amethyst 29
Ammonite fossil 29
Andean condor 15
Anemones
    Beadlet anemone 23
    Jewel anemone 20
    Magnificent sea anemone 19
    Pacific strawberry anemone 19
    Pom-pom anemone 20
    Snakelocks anemone 20
Angora goat 24
Angora kid 24
Animal bones 17
Animal dung 16
Anna's hummingbird nest 7
Antarctic krill 18
Antarctic pearlwort 18
Anteater, Lesser 11
Antelope jackrabbit 17
Ants
    Army ant 11
    Black garden ant 6
    Sahara desert ant 17
Apes
    Sumatran orangutan 11
    Western gorilla 12
Appaloosa mule 24
Apple 9
Apple pips 9
Apple tree 28
Aquamarine 29
Arabian jasmine 10
Arboreal termite nest 8

Arctic char 18
Arctic fox 18
Arctic hare 18
Arctic woolly bear caterpillar 18
Arctic woolly bear moth 18
Argillite 15
Arizona blond tarantula 17
Arizona coral snake 17
Armadillo, Nine-banded 16
Army ant 11
Asparagus 25
Atlantic blue marlin 20
Atlantic puffin 23
Atlantic walrus 18
Atlas cedar 13
Atlas cedar cone 9
Atlas cedar leaves 9
Australian baobab 28
Avalanche 18
Avocado 9
Avocado stone 9
Axolotl 21
Aye-aye 12
Ayers rock / Uluru 17

B

Baboon, Hamadryas 16
Badger, European 6
Baikal seal 21
Bald eagle nest 7
Bald-faced hornet 8
Bald-faced hornet's nest 8
Banana plant 12
Bananas 12
Bank vole 5
Barley 24
Barn owl 24
Barrel jellyfish 20
Basil 26
Basking shark 19
Bat-eared fox 16
Bay tree 27
Baya weaver nest 7
Beach cliff 23
Beadlet anemone 23
Bearded bellflower 15
Bearded seal 18
Bears
    American black bear 13
    Grizzly bear 13
    Himalayan brown bear 15
    Polar bear 18
Beaver dam 22
Beaver, North American 22
Beavertail cactus 17
Bees
    European honeybee 6
    Garden bumblebee 6
    Shrill carder bee 5
    Stingless Mayan bee 11
Belemnite fossil 29
Bell heather 13
Beluga whale 18
Bengal tiger 11
Big bluestem grass 16
Big galleta 17
Bilberry 13
Bird's-foot trefoil 5
Birds
    Abacot ranger duck 24
    Adélie penguin 18

Alpine swift 15
American flamingo 21
American robin 6
Andean condor 15
Atlantic puffin 23
Barn owl 24
Black-and-yellow broadbill 11
Black-capped lory 11
Blue jay 14
Blue-and-yellow macaw 11
Blue-winged parrotlet 16
Bourbon red turkey 24
Broad-billed hummingbird 17
Budgerigar 16
Common bullfinch 5
Common chaffinch 5
Common kestrel 16
Common kingfisher 22
Common moorhen 21
Common ostrich 16
Common pheasant 24
Common shelduck 23
Common starling 6
Common whitethroat 5
Common wood pigeon 6
Crimson-breasted flowerpecker 11
Dark-eyed junco 6
Elf owl 17
Embden goose 24
Emperor penguin 18
Eurasian blue tit 5
Eurasian wigeon 21
European greenfinch 6
European herring gull 23
European robin 6
European wren 5
Gambel's quail 17
Gilded flicker 17
Golden eagle 15
Great crested grebe 21
Great hornbill 12
Great white pelican 23
Grey heron 22
Grey partridge 24
Harpy eagle 12
Helmeted guineafowl 24
House sparrow 6
Keel-billed toucan 12
Ladder-backed woodpecker 17
Laughing kookaburra 6
Lewis's woodpecker 13
Lilac-breasted roller 16
Long-eared owl 13
Long-tailed tit 6
Malachite kingfisher 22
Mallard 21
Mandarin duck 22
Mealy Amazon 11
Mountain quail 15
Moustached babbler 11
Mute swan 21
Noisy miner 6
Northern cardinal 14
Northern fulmar 18
Northern pintail 21
Oriental dwarf kingfisher 12
Orpington hen 24
Painted stork 22
Pileated woodpecker 14
Red crossbill 13
Red-billed hornbill 16
Resplendent quetzal 12

Rock ptarmigan 18
Rough-legged buzzard 18
Ruffed grouse 14
Saddle-billed stork 16
Sharp-shinned hawk 13
Short-eared owl 16
Snow petrel 18
Snowy owl 18
Song thrush 5
Southern cassowary 12
Spectacled owl 12
Spicebush swallowtail 14
Spotted owl 13
Sussex cock 24
Tawny owl 6
Tufted duck 21
Turquoise-browed motmot 16
Vulturine guineafowl 16
Wandering albatross 18
Wilson's bird-of-paradise 11
Yellowhammer 5
Bison, American 16
Black cherry plum 28
Black garden ant 6
Black morel mushroom 13
Black pepper 25
Black poplar 27
Black slug 6
Black-and-white ruffed lemur 11
Black-and-yellow broadbill 11
Black-capped lory 11
Black-lip pearl oyster 19
Black-tailed prairie dog 16
Blackberry bramble 5
Blackthorn 5
Blue catfish 22
Blue discus 22
Blue jacaranda 27
Blue jay 14
Blue jay nest 14
Blue morpho butterfly 8
Blue morpho butterfly's eggs 8
Blue mussel 20
Blue whale 19
Blue wildebeest 16
Blue-and-yellow macaw 11
Blue-fronted Amazon feather 7
Blue-spotted stingray 20
Blue-winged parrotlet 16
Boer goat 24
Bongo 11
Boojum tree 28
Boomslang snake 16
Border collie 24
Bottlenose dolphin, Common 19
Bourbon red turkey 24
Bowhead whale 18
Bracken 13
Brazil nut tree 11
Breadfruit 12
British Landrace pig 24
British Landrace piglet 24
Broad-billed hummingbird 17
Broccoli 25
Brook trout 15
Brown long-eared bat 5
Brown rat 6
Brown-throated sloth 11
Bubble snail 19
Bubblegum coral 19
Budgerigar 16
Buffalo, African 16

Buffalo grass 16
Bugs
    American cockroach 8
    Arctic woolly bear caterpillar 18
    Arizona blond tarantula 17
    Army ant 11
    Bald-faced hornet 8
    Black garden ant 6
    Black slug 6
    Bumblebee millipede 8
    Camel spider 17
    Cathedral termite 8
    Cinnabar caterpillar 8
    Colorado beetle 8
    Common earthworm 6
    Common scorpionfly 5
    Common wasp 6
    Common woodlouse 6
    Daring jumping spider 8
    Diadem spider 5
    Dung beetle 16
    Eastern lubber grasshopper 8
    Eastern striped cricket 8
    European honeybee 6
    European paper wasp 8
    Florida blue centipede 8
    Forest tent caterpillar 8
    Garden banded snail 5
    Garden bumblebee 6
    Garden snail 6
    Giant hairy scorpion 17
    Golden ground beetle 5
    Goliath bird-eater spider 11
    Grass cross spider 8
    Great diving beetle 21
    Green lacewing 8
    Green shield bug 8
    Green tiger beetle 8
    Hercules beetle 11
    Housefly 6
    Juniper webworm 13
    Larch silkworm 13
    Lesser water boatman 21
    Madagascar giraffe weevil 11
    March brown mayfly 22
    Meadow grasshopper 5
    Mexican red-kneed tarantula 8
    Monarch caterpillar 8
    Mosquito 8
    Oak marble gall wasp 8
    Picasso bug 8
    Praying mantis 8
    Rainbow stag beetle 11
    Sahara desert ant 17
    Seven-spot ladybird 6
    Shrill carder bee 5
    Speckled bush-cricket 6
    Spotted cranefly 8
    Spotted longhorn beetle 14
    Spotted oleander caterpillar 8
    Stag beetle 5
    Stingless Mayan bee 11
    Stone centipede 6
    Two-lined spittlebug 8
    Yellow potter wasp 8
Bulb 10
Bull kelp 20
Bumblebee, Garden 6
Bumblebee millipede 8
Bumblebee poison frog 12
Bunny ears cactus 10
Burdock burrs 9
Burnet moth's cocoon 8
Burrows
    Marmot burrow 15
    Rabbit warren 5

Butterflies
    Blue morpho butterfly 8
    Comma butterfly 5
    Gatekeeper butterfly 5
    Holly blue butterfly 6
    Monarch butterfly 8
    Mountain fritillary butterfly 15
    Orange tip butterfly 5
    Peacock butterfly 6
    Phoebus Apollo butterfly 15
    Purple-edged copper
      butterfly 15
    Queen Alexandra's birdwing
      butterfly 11
    Red Admiral butterfly 6
    Spicebush swallowtail 14
Butternut squash 25
Buttress roots 12

C
Cabbage palmetto leaf 9
Cactuses
    Beavertail cactus 17
    Bunny ears cactus 10
    Fishhook barrel cactus 17
    Peruvian apple cactus 10
    Rainbow pincushion 10
    Saguaro cactus 17
    Teddy-bear cholla 17
    Whiskerbush cactus 10
Camel spider 17
Camel thorn 17
Canada lynx 13
Canada red chokecherry 27
Canadian bunchberry 13
Canadian hemlock 13
Candelabra tree 16
Canyon 17
Capybara 22
Carnation coral 19
Carrot 25
Cassava 24
Cathedral termite 8
Cathedral termite mound 8
Caviar 25
Celeriac 25
Central American agouti 11
Cetti's warbler nest 7
Chaffinch, Common 5
Chaffinch nest 5
Chalk 29
Chameleon, Parson's 12
Cheetah, South African 16
Cherry 9
Cherry stone 9
Cherry tomatoes 25
Chick, Orpington 24
Chicken egg 25
Chickpeas 26
Chinese paperbark maple bark 28
Chrysanthemum 10
Chukar partridge feather 7
Cinnabar caterpillar 8
Cinnabar chanterelle 14
Cinnabar moth 8
Cinnamon 25
Cloudberry 13
Cloves 25
Coal 29
Cockroach, American 8
Cocoa pod 12
Coconut 23
Coconut palm 23
Cod 26
Coffee beans 25

Colorado beetle 8
Comma butterfly 5
Common ash leaf 9
Common bearberry 18
Common beech 14
Common bluebell 5
Common bottlenose dolphin 19
Common bullfinch 5
Common chaffinch 5
Common cuttlefish 20
Common daisy 6
Common dandelion 6
Common darter dragonfly 21
Common duckweed 21
Common earthworm 6
Common foxglove 5
Common frog 6
Common golden thistle 10
Common greenshield lichen 14
Common hawthorn 27
Common hippopotamus 22
Common honeysuckle 5
Common hyacinth 10
Common iguana 12
Common ivy 6
Common juniper 15
Common kestrel 16
Common kingfisher 22
Common laburnum 6
Common limpet 23
Common lobster 20
Common moorhen 21
Common murre egg 7
Common ostrich 16
Common pear leaf 9
Common pheasant 24
Common privet 5
Common rabbit 5
Common reed bunting egg 7
Common rudd 22
Common scorpionfly 5
Common sea urchin 23
Common shelduck 23
Common shrew 6
Common starling 6
Common sundew leaf 9
Common toad 14
Common walnut tree 28
Common warthog 16
Common wasp 6
Common water hyacinth 21
Common wheat 24
Common whitethroat 5
Common wood pigeon 6
Common woodlouse 6
Common zinnia 10
Conker 9
Coral reef 19
Coriander 26
Cornflower 10
Cotton 24
Cougar 15
Crab 26
Crab apple 5
Crack willow leaf 9
Crimson-breasted flowerpecker 11
Cuckoo flower 5
Curly waterweed 21
Cuttlebone 23
Cycad cone 9
Cyclamen 10

D
Daffodil 10
Daisy, Common 6

Dandelion clock 9
Dandelion, Common 6
Daring jumping spider 8
Dark-eyed junco 6
Dawn redwood 14
Dawn redwood leaves 9
Deep sea anglerfish 20
Deer
    Alaskan moose 18
    Fallow deer 14
    Svalbard reindeer 18
    White-tailed deer 14
Deodar cedar 27
Desert fan palm 17
Desert pavement 17
Desert sunflower 17
Desert willow 17
Devil's matchstick lichen 14
Diadem spider 5
Diamond 29
Dolphins
    Amazon river dolphin 22
    Common bottlenose
      dolphin 19
    Short-beaked common
      dolphin 23
Domestic cat 6
Dormouse, Hazel 5
Dormouse nest 5
Douglas fir 13
Dragon blood tree 27
Dragonflies
    Common darter dragonfly 21
    Southern hawker dragonfly 21
Driftwood 23
Dromedary 17
Ducks
    Abacot ranger duck 24
    Common shelduck 23
    Mallard 21
    Mandarin duck 22
    Northern pintail 21
    Tufted duck 21
Dung beetle 16
Dunnock egg 7
Durian 12
Dust devil 17
Dwarf sea snake 20
Dwarf seahorse 19
Dwarf willow 15

E
Eagle, Golden 15
Early purple orchid 5
Earthworm, Common 6
Eastern chipmunk 14
Eastern lubber grasshopper 8
Eastern redbud seed pod 9
Eastern striped cricket 8
Echinoid fossil 29
Eggs
    American robin egg 7
    Blue morpho butterfly's eggs 8
    Chicken egg 25
    Common murre egg 7
    Common reed bunting egg 7
    Dunnock egg 7
    Elegant crested tinamou egg 7
    Emu egg 7
    Eurasian sparrowhawk egg 7
    European buzzard egg 7
    Golden eagle egg 7
    Goose egg 25
    Green lacewing's eggs 8
    Green shield bug's eggs 8

Guira cuckoo egg 7
House wren egg 7
Maran chicken egg 7
Mistle thrush egg 7
Ostrich egg 7
Quail egg 25
Red-winged blackbird egg
Southern cassowary egg
Egyptian blue lotus 21
Elder flower 5
Elegant crested tinamou egg
Elegant sea star 20
Elephant, Namibian desert
Elf owl 17
Embden goose 24
Emerald 29
Emerald tree boa 12
Emperor newt 21
Emperor penguin 18
Emperor tamarin 12
Emu egg 7
Enchanter's nightshade 14
English holly 14
English oak 14
English oak leaf 9
English yew 27
Ermine 18
Eurasian blue tit 5
Eurasian coot nest 7
Eurasian penduline tit nest 7
Eurasian sparrowhawk egg
Eurasian wigeon 21
Eurasian wolf 13
European ash 27
European badger 6
European beech 27
European bitterling 22
European buzzard egg 7
European greenfinch 6
European hare 24
European harvest mouse 5
European hedgehog 5
European herring gull 23
European honeybee 6
European jay feather 7
European mole 6
European painted top shell 2
European paper wasp 8
European pine marten 13
European plaice 7
European pond terrapin 21
European robin 6
European wren 5

F
Fairy chimney 17
Fallow deer 14
False bird-of-paradise 11
Feathers
    Alexandrine parakeet
      feather 7
    Blue-fronted Amazon
      feather 7
    Chukar partridge feather 7
    European jay feather 7
    Flamingo feather 7
    Golden oriole feather 7
    Golden-headed quetzal
      feather 7
    Great spotted woodpecker
      feather 7
    King bird-of-paradise
      feather 7
    Mallard feather 7
    Mandarin duck feather 7

Mute swan feather 7
Ostrich feather 7
Peacock feather 7
Pheasant feather 7
Red-crested turaco feather 7
Screech owl feather 7
nec fox 17
d maple seeds 9
tree 28
ess porpoise 19
shrimp 20
bone beard lichen 13
hook barrel cactus 17
d horse 15
tail surgeonfish 19
mboyant tree 28
mingo, American 21
mingo feather 7
x 24
t 29
ida blue centipede 8
ida pompano 23
ver of the Andes 15
vering cherry 6
vering rush 21
vers
Alpenrose 15
Alpine rock-jasmine 15
Alpine snowbell 15
Antarctic pearlwort 18
Arabian jasmine 10
Bearded bellflower 15
Bell heather 13
Bird's-foot trefoil 5
Chrysanthemum 10
Common bluebell 14
Common daisy 6
Common dandelion 6
Common foxglove 5
Common golden thistle 10
Common honeysuckle 5
Common hyacinth 10
Common laburnum 6
Common privet 5
Common water hyacinth 21
Common zinnia 10
Cornflower 10
Cuckoo flower 5
Cyclamen 10
Daffodil 10
Desert sunflower 17
Early purple orchid 5
Egyptian blue lotus 21
Elder flower 5
Enchanter's nightshade 14
False bird-of-paradise 11
Flax 24
Flower of the Andes 15
Flowering rush 21
Freesia 10
French marigold 10
Frogbit 21
Garden tulip 10
Glory-of-the-snow 15
Golden samphire 23
Grass of the dew 10
Great willowherb 22
Greater butterfly orchid 14
Guelder rose 5
Hedge bedstraw 5
Hop hornbeam catkin 14
Indian lotus 21
Iris 10
Lavender 10
Lesser celandine 14
Lilac 10

Lily-of-the-valley 10
Long-flowered crocus 10
Meadow buttercup 5
Milk thistle 10
Moth orchid 10
Mountain cornflower 15
Mountain everlasting 15
Ocotillo flower 17
Palm lily 10
Passion fruit flower 11
Peacock flower 11
Purple loosestrife 22
Rafflesia 11
Rapeseed 24
Red ginger 10
Rose 10
Sanicle 13
Sea pink 23
Silky phacelia 15
Silver vase bromeliad 12
Small teasel 22
Southern arrowwood 14
Stargazer lily 10
Starry saxifrage 15
Sunflower 10
Sweet pea 10
Traveller's joy 5
Victoria waterlily 11
Water arum 10
Water crowfoot 21
Water soldier 21
White asphodel 15
White clover 6
Wild-sage 10
Wood forget-me-not 10
Yellow archangel 5
Yellow horned poppy 23
Yellow iris 22
Yellow loosestrife 22
Fly agaric mushroom 13
Fool's gold 29
Forceps butterflyfish 19
Forest tent caterpillar 8
Forest tent caterpillar moth 8
Fossil shark's tooth 23
Fossil wood 29
Fox, Red 6
Freesia 10
French marigold 10
Freshwater pearl mussel 22
Friesian cow 24
Frog, Common 6
Frogbit 21
Frost's bolete mushroom 14
Frozen waterfall 18
Fruit
  Apple 9
  Avocado 9
  Bananas 12
  Bilberry 13
  Blackberry bramble 5
  Breadfruit 12
  Canadian bunchberry 13
  Cherry 9
  Cherry tomatoes 25
  Cloudberry 13
  Coconut 23
  Common bearberry 18
  Crab apple 5
  Durian 12
  Grapes 25
  Guava fruit 12
  Jojoba fruit 17
  Kiwi fruit 25
  Lemon 25
  Lime 26

  Mango 25
  Orange 25
  Papaya fruit 12
  Passion fruit 26
  Peach 9
  Pear 26
  Plum 26
  Watermelon 26
  Wild strawberries 5
Funnel-web spider's web 8

G

Gambel's quail 17
Garden banded snail 5
Garden bumblebee 6
Garden snail 6
Garden tulip 10
Garlic 25
Garnet 29
Garnierite 29
Gatekeeper butterfly 5
Geode 29
Gerenuk 16
German shepherd 24
Giant airplant 12
Giant hairy scorpion 17
Giant hermit crab 20
Giant kelp 20
Giant quiver tree 27
Giant redwood 27
Gila monster 17
Gilded flicker 17
Ginger root 25
Glacial squid 20
Glacier 18
Glacier cave 18
Glory-of-the-snow 15
Goat, Angora 24
Gold 29
Golden alpine salamander 15
Golden eagle 15
Golden eagle egg 7
Golden ground beetle 5
Golden jelly fungus 14
Golden lion tamarin 12
Golden oriole feather 7
Golden samphire 23
Golden-headed quetzal feather 7
Goliath bird-eater spider 11
Goose egg 25
Gopher tortoise 13
Gorilla nest 12
Gorilla, Western 12
Grandidier's baobab 27
Granite 29
Grapes 25
Grass cross spider 8
Grass of the dew 10
Grasshopper, Meadow 5
Great Basin Bristlecone pine 28
Great crested grebe 21
Great diving beetle 21
Great hairy willowherb seed pod 9
Great hammerhead shark 19
Great hornbill 12
Great ramshorn 21
Great reedmace 22
Great spotted woodpecker feather 7
Great white pelican 23
Great white shark 19
Great willowherb 22
Greater butterfly orchid 14
Green anaconda 22

Green lacewing 8
Green lacewing's eggs 8
Green sea turtle 20
Green shield bug 8
Green shield bug's eggs 8
Green tiger beetle 8
Greenschist 15
Grey heron 22
Grey partridge 24
Grey squirrel 6
Grizzly bear 13
Ground pangolin 16
Guava fruit 12
Guava tree 12
Guelder rose 5
Guira cuckoo egg 7

H

Haddock 26
Hamadryas baboon 16
Hampshire pig 24
Harbour porpoise 23
Harpy eagle 12
Harris hawk nest 7
Hazel dormouse 5
Hazelnuts 26
Hedge bedstraw 5
Helmeted guineafowl 24
Hen, Orpington 24
Hercules beetle 11
Herring 26
Highland pony 24
Himalayan brown bear 15
Hippopotamus, Common 22
Holly blue butterfly 6
Holly leaf 9
Honey 26
Honey locust 27
Honeybee, European 6
Hop hornbeam catkin 14
Hopkin's rose 20
Horse chestnut leaf 9
Horse chestnut tree 27
Horses
  Fjord horse 15
  Highland pony 24
  Shire foal 24
  Shire horse 24
House mouse 6
House sparrow 6
House wren egg 7
Housefly 6
Hummingbird hawk-moth 5
Humpback whale 18
Hydrothermal vents 19
Hyena, Spotted 16

I

Ice floe 18
Iceberg 18
Iceland moss 15
Icicles 18
Iguana, Common 12
Impala 16
Indian desert jird 17
Indian lotus 21
Indigo milk cap mushroom 14
Indo-Pacific sailfish 20
Iris 10
Ivy, Common 6

J

Jackalberry tree 16

Jade 29
Jade plant 10
Jaguar 11
Japanese cherry 27
Japanese seabream 20
Jersey calf 24
Jersey cow 24
Jewel anemone 20
Johnson's sea cucumber 20
Jojoba fruit 17
Joshua tree 17
Juniper webworm 13

K

Kangaroo grass 16
Kangaroo, Red 17
Kapok tree 11
Keel-billed toucan 12
Kidney beans 26
King bird-of-paradise feather 7
King palm 28
King ragworm 20
Kiwi fruit 25
Knobbed whelk egg case 23
Knotted wrack 23
Kokerboom 28
Kopje 16

L

Ladder-backed woodpecker 17
Lamb, Merino 24
Lapis lazuli 29
Lappet-faced vulture nest 7
Larch silkworm 13
Laughing kookaburra 6
Lavender 10
Leaf buds 9
Leaf skeleton 9
Leatherback sea turtle 23
Lemon 25
Lentils 26
Lesser anteater 11
Lesser celandine 14
Lesser water boatman 21
Lettuce 25
Lewis's woodpecker 13
Leyland cypress 6
Lianas 12
Lilac 10
Lilac-breasted roller 16
Lily-of-the-valley 10
Lime 26
Limestone 29
Limey petticoat 20
Lined seahorse 19
Lion, West African 16
Lion's mane jellyfish 20
Little brown bat 14
Little grebe nest 7
Livingston's Cichlid 21
Lobster 26
Lobster, Common 20
London plane 27
Long-eared owl 13
Long-flowered crocus 10
Long-tailed tit 6

M

Macadamia nuts 26
Mackerel 26
Mackerel icefish 18
Madagascar giraffe weevil 11
Magnetic termite mound 8

Magnificent sea anemone   19
Maidenhair tree   28
Maidenhair tree leaf   9
Maize   24
Malachite kingfisher   22
Malay fruit bat   11
Mallard   21
Mallard feather   7
Mandarin duck   22
Mandarin duck feather   7
Mandrill   11
Manganese nodule   19
Mango   25
Maran chicken egg   7
Marble   29
March brown mayfly   22
Marmot burrow   15
Masai giraffe   16
Meadow buttercup   5
Meadow grasshopper   5
Mealy Amazon   11
Mediterranean cypress   27
Mediterranean monk seal   23
Meerkat   17
Merino lamb   24
Merino sheep   24
Mexican red-kneed tarantula   8
Mice
    European harvest mouse   5
    Hazel dormouse   5
    House mouse   6
    Striped field mouse   24
    Wood mouse   6
Milk   25
Milk thistle   10
Milkweed seed pod   9
Mint   26
Mistle thrush egg   7
Mole, European   6
Monarch butterfly   8
Monarch butterfly's chrysalis   8
Monarch caterpillar   8
Money spider's web   8
Monkey cup pitcher plant   12
Monkey puzzle tree   28
Monkey-bread tree   16
Monkeys
    Emperor tamarin   12
    Golden lion tamarin   12
    Hamadryas baboon   16
    Mandrill   11
    Woolly monkey   12
Montezuma oropendola nest   7
Moon snail egg collar   23
Moose, Alaskan   18
Mosquito   8
Moth orchid   10
Moths
    Arctic woolly bear moth   18
    Cinnabar moth   8
    Forest tent moth   8
    Hummingbird hawk-moth   5
    Poplar hawk-moth   14
    Spotted oleander caterpillar
    moth   8
Mount Etna broom   28
Mountain cabbage tree   28
Mountain cornflower   15
Mountain everlasting   15
Mountain fritillary butterfly   15
Mountain hemlock   15
Mountain quail   15
Moustached babbler   11
Mushrooms   25
Muskrat   21
Mustard seeds   9

Mute swan   21
Mute swan feather   7

N
Namibian desert elephant   17
Narwhal   18
Natural arch   23
Needle ice   18
Nests
    American cliff swallow nest   7
    Anna's hummingbird nest   7
    Bald eagle nest   7
    Bald-faced hornet's nest   8
    Baya weaver nest   7
    Blue jay nest   14
    Cetti's warbler nest   7
    Chaffinch nest   5
    Dormouse nest   5
    Eurasian coot nest   7
    Eurasian penduline tit nest   7
    Gorilla nest   12
    Harris hawk nest   7
    Lappet-faced vulture nest   7
    Little grebe nest   7
    Montezuma oropendola nest   7
    Orangutan nest   11
    Ovenbird nest   7
    Paper wasp's nest   8
    Potter wasp's nests   8
    Sea turtle nest   23
    Sociable weaver nests   7
    Song thrush nest   5
Netted dog whelk shell   23
New Zealand cushion plant   15
New Zealand sea lion   20
Nile crocodile   22
Nine-banded armadillo   16
Noisy miner   6
Norfolk Island pine leaves   9
North American beaver   22
North American porcupine   13
North American raccoon   6
North American river otter   22
Northern cardinal   14
Northern fulmar   18
Northern minke whale   23
Northern pike   22
Northern pintail   21
Northern red oak   28
Northern water snake   21
Northern water vole   22
Norway lemming   18
Norway spruce cone   9
Norway spruce leaves   9

O
Oak marble gall wasp   8
Oak marble galls   8
Oasis   17
Ocelot   11
Ocotillo flower   17
Octopus, Ruby   20
Ohio buckeye seed   9
Okapi   11
Olive tree   28
Onion   25
Opal   29
Opalescent squid   20
Orange   25
Orange clownfish   19
Orange puffball sponge   20
Orange sea lichen   23
Orange tip butterfly   5
Orangutan nest   11

Orangutan, Sumatran   11
Orbweaver spider's web   8
Oriental dwarf kingfisher   12
Orpington chick   24
Orpington hen   24
Ostrich, Common   16
Ostrich egg   7
Ostrich feather   7
Ostrich fern   10
Otter, North American river   22
Ovenbird nest   7
Owl pellet   13
Owls
    Barn owl   24
    Elf owl   17
    Long-eared owl   13
    Short-eared owl   16
    Snowy owl   18
    Spectacled owl   12
    Spotted owl   13
    Tawny owl   6
Ozark minnow   22

P
Pacific strawberry anemone   19
Painted stork   22
Palm lily   10
Pampas grass   16
Papaya fruit   12
Papaya tree   12
Paper birch bark   28
Paper wasp's nest   8
Parson's chameleon   12
Passion fruit   26
Passion fruit flower   11
Patagonian toothfish   18
Peach   9
Peach stone   9
Peacock bass   22
Peacock butterfly   6
Peacock feather   7
Peacock flower   11
Peanuts   26
Pear   26
Pear tree   28
Pecans   26
Penguins
    Adélie penguin   18
    Emperor penguin   18
Penitentes snow formation   18
Penny bun mushroom   13
Peridot   29
Peruvian apple cactus   10
Petal   10
Pheasant, Common   24
Pheasant feather   7
Phoebus Apollo butterfly   15
Picasso bug   8
Pigeon, Common wood   6
Pignut hickory   27
Pileated woodpecker   14
Pillow lava   19
Pine mushroom   13
Pine nuts   26
Pipistrelle bat   6
Piranha, Red-bellied   22
Pistachios   26
Pixie cup lichen   15
Plains zebra   16
Platypus   22
Plum   26
Poitou donkey   24
Polar bear   18
Pom-pom anemone   20
Poplar hawk-moth   14

Potatoes   24
Potter wasp's nests   8
Prawns   26
Praying mantis   8
Provence donkey   24
Provence foal   24
Prussian carp   22
Puffin, Atlantic   23
Pumice   29
Pumpkin   24
Pumpkin seeds   9
Purple loosestrife   22
Purple sea star   20
Purple-edged copper butterfly   15
Python, African rock   16

Q
Quail egg   25
Quail, Mountain   15
Quaking aspen   15
Queen Alexandra's birdwing
    butterfly   11
Queen angelfish   19
Queen conch shell   23
Queen of the Andes   15
Queensland kauri pine   13

R
Rabbit, Common   5
Rabbit warren   5
Raccoon, North American   6
Radicchio   25
Rafflesia   11
Rainbow eucalyptus bark   28
Rainbow pincushion   10
Rainbow stag beetle   11
Rapeseed   24
Real fan palm   28
Red Admiral butterfly   6
Red beryl   29
Red cecropia   11
Red crossbill   13
Red fox   6
Red ginger   10
Red jasper   29
Red kangaroo   17
Red mangrove   11
Red pepper   25
Red sea fan   19
Red-bellied piranha   22
Red-billed hornbill   16
Red-crested turaco feather   7
Red-eyed tree frog   12
Red-winged blackbird egg   7
Redclaw crayfish   22
Redside dace   21
Reindeer lichen   18
Resplendent quetzal   12
Rhinoceros, Southern white   16
Rhodonite   29
Rice   26
Rice plant   24
Rock pinnacle   15
Rock ptarmigan   18
Rocket   26
Rocky Mountain elk   15
Rocky Mountain goat   15
Rocky outcrop   15
Root ginger   25
Roots   10
Rose   10
Rose quartz   29
Rosehip   5
Rosemary   26

Rough-legged buzzard   18
Rowan leaf   9
Rowan tree   27
Royal angelfish   19
Ruby octopus   20
Ruffed grouse   14
Russian larch   27
Rye   24

S
Saddle-billed stork   16
Saguaro cactus   17
Sahara desert ant   17
Salmon   26
Saltwater crocodile   20
Sand   23
Sand cat   17
Sand dollar   23
Sand dune   17
Sandstone   29
Sandstorm   17
Sanicle   13
Sapphire   29
Scallop shell   23
Scarlet oak   27
Scorpion, Giant hairy   17
Scots pine   27
Scottish blackface sheep   24
Screech owl feather   7
Sea apple   19
Sea bass   26
Sea cave   23
Sea kale   23
Sea lettuce   23
Sea pink   23
Sea salt   25
Sea stack   23
Sea star fossil   29
Sea turtle nest   23
Sea urchin, Common   23
Seamount   19
Seaweed   26
Seed fern fossil   29
Serpentine   29
Serval   16
Sesame seeds   9
Seven-spot ladybird   6
Shark egg case   23
Sharks
    Basking shark   19
    Great hammerhead
    shark   19
    Great white shark   19
    Whale shark   19
Sharp-shinned hawk   13
Shed deer antler   14
Shed snake skin   17
Shingle   23
Shire foal   24
Shire horse   24
Shoal weed   20
Short-beaked common
    dolphin   23
Short-eared owl   16
Shrew, Common   6
Shrill carder bee   5
Siberian tiger   18
Sidewinder   17
Silky phacelia   15
Silver   29
Silver birch   14
Silver fir   27
Silver spruce   15
Silver tree   27
Silver vase bromeliad   12

Slate 29
Sloth, Brown-throated 11
Slug, Black 6
Small teasel 22
Smooth newt 21
Snail shell 6
Snakelocks anemone 20
Snakes
   African rock python 16
   Arizona coral snake 17
   Boomslang snake 16
   Dwarf sea snake 20
   Emerald tree boa 12
   Green anaconda 22
   Northern water snake 21
   Sidewinder 17
   Timber rattlesnake 14
Snow chimney 18
Snow leopard 15
Snow petrel 18
Snowflakes 18
Snowy mespilus 28
Snowy owl 18
Sociable weaver nests 7
Soft rime 18
Soft shield fern 22
Song thrush 5
Song thrush nest 5
Sorghum 24
South African cheetah 16
Southern arrowwood 14
Southern brown bandicoot 16
Southern cassowary 12
Southern cassowary egg 7
Southern hawker dragonfly 21
Southern white rhinoceros 16
Soya beans 24
Speckled bush-cricket 6
Spectacled owl 12
Sperm whale 19
Spicebush swallowtail 14
Spider plant 10
Spiders
   Arizona blond tarantula 17
   Camel spider 17
   Daring jumping spider 8
   Diadem spider 5
   Goliath bird-eater spider 11
   Grass cross spider 8
   Mexican red-kneed
   tarantula 8
Spinach 25
Spittlebug foam 8
Spotted cranefly 8
Spotted hyena 16
Spotted longhorn beetle 14
Spotted oleander caterpillar 8
Spotted oleander caterpillar
moth 8
Spotted owl 13
Spotted reef crab 20
Spotted salamander 14

Spring onions 25
Squirrel's drey 13
Stag beetle 5
Stalactite 29
Stalagmite 29
Star anise 25
Star grass 20
Stargazer lily 10
Starling, Common 6
Starry saxifrage 15
Stem 10
Stinging nettle 5
Stingless Mayan bee 11
Stingray, Blue-spotted 20
Stone centipede 6
Stone pine bark 28
Stove-pipe sponge 19
Strawberries, Wild 5
Striped field mouse 24
Striped skunk 14
Submarine volcano 19
Sugar beet 24
Sugar cane 25
Sugar maple 28
Sugar maple leaf 9
Sumatran orangutan 11
Sunapee golden trout 15
Sunflower 10
Sunflower seeds 9
Sussex cock 24
Svalbard reindeer 18
Swan mussel 21
Swan, Mute 21
Sweet orange tree 27
Sweet pea 10
Sweetgum leaf 9
Sycamore tree 27

T

Tall fescue grass 6
Tawny owl 6
Tea leaves 25
Teak 28
Teddy-bear cholla 17
Thorny dragon 17
Thunderegg 29
Thunderstorm 12
Tiger, Bengal 11
Timber rattlesnake 14
Toad, Common 14
Toddy palm 27
Tomatoes, Cherry 25
Topaz 29
Tourmaline 29
Traveller's joy 5
Tree aloe 28
Trees
   African mulberry 27
   American elm 27
   Apple tree 28
   Atlas cedar 13

Australian baobab 28
Bay tree 27
Black cherry plum 28
Black poplar 27
Blue jacaranda 27
Boojum tree 28
Brazil nut tree 11
Camel thorn 17
Canada red chokecherry 27
Canadian hemlock 13
Candelabra tree 16
Coconut palm 23
Common beech 14
Common hawthorn 27
Common juniper 15
Common walnut tree 28
Dawn redwood 14
Deodar cedar 27
Desert fan palm 17
Desert willow 17
Douglas fir 13
Dragon blood tree 27
English oak 14
English yew 27
European ash 27
European beech 27
Fig tree 28
Flamboyant tree 28
Flowering cherry 6
Giant quiver tree 27
Giant redwood 27
Grandidier's baobab 27
Great Basin Bristlecone
pine 28
Guava tree 12
Honey locust 27
Horse chestnut tree 27
Jackalberry tree 16
Japanese cherry 27
Joshua tree 17
Kapok tree 11
King palm 28
Kokerboom 28
Leyland cypress 6
London plane 27
Maidenhair tree 28
Mediterranean cypress 27
Monkey puzzle tree 28
Monkey-bread tree 16
Mount Etna broom 28
Mountain cabbage tree 28
Mountain hemlock 15
Northern red oak 28
Olive tree 28
Papaya tree 12
Pear tree 28
Pignut hickory 27
Quaking aspen 15
Queen of the Andes 15
Queensland kauri pine 13
Real fan palm 28
Red cecropia 11

Red mangrove 11
Rowan tree 27
Russian larch 27
Scarlet oak 27
Scots pine 27
Silver birch 14
Silver fir 27
Silver spruce 15
Silver tree 27
Snowy mespilus 28
Sugar maple 28
Sweet orange tree 27
Sycamore tree 27
Teak 28
Toddy palm 27
Tree aloe 28
Tualang tree 12
Umbrella thorn acacia 16
Umbrella tree 27
Utah juniper 28
Walking palm 11
Weeping fig 10
Weeping golden willow 28
Western hemlock 28
Wollemi pine 28
Yew plum pine 13
Trilobite fossil 29
Trout 26
Truffles 25
Tualang tree 12
Tufted duck 21
Tulip tree leaf 9
Tumbleweed 17
Tuna 26
Turkey tail mushroom 14
Turquoise 29
Turquoise-browed motmot 16
Two-lined spittlebug 8

U

Uluru / Ayers rock 17
Umbrella thorn acacia 16
Umbrella tree 27
Utah juniper 28

V

Venus comb 20
Venus flytrap 10
Victoria waterlily 11
Virginia opossum 14
Vulturine guineafowl 16

W

Walking palm 11
Walnut 26
Walrus, Atlantic 18
Wandering albatross 18
Warthog, Common 16
Wasp, Common 6

Water 25
Water arum 10
Water crowfoot 21
Water soldier 21
Waterhole 16
Watermelon 26
Watermelon snow 18
Weeping fig 10
Weeping golden willow 28
West African lion 16
West Indian manatee 20
Western gorilla 12
Western hemlock 28
Western swordfern 13
Whale shark 19
Whales
   Beluga whale 18
   Blue whale 19
   Bowhead whale 18
   Humpback whale 18
   Narwhal 18
   Northern minke whale 23
   Sperm whale 19
Whiskerbush cactus 10
White ash seed 9
White asphodel 15
White clover 6
White cottongrass 18
White-tailed deer 14
Wild boar 14
Wild strawberries 5
Wild-sage 10
Willow emerald damselfly 21
Wilson's bird-of-paradise 11
Wolf, Eurasian 13
Wollemi pine 28
Wood forget-me-not 10
Wood mouse 6
Woodlouse, Common 6
Woolly monkey 12

Y

Yellow archangel 5
Yellow groove bamboo 10
Yellow horned poppy 23
Yellow iris 22
Yellow loosestrife 22
Yellow perch 21
Yellow potter wasp 8
Yellow seahorse 23
Yellow-bellied slider 22
Yellowfin goatfish 23
Yellowhammer 5
Yew plum pine 13

Z

Zebra, Plains 16
Zebra plant leaf 9
Zebra seahorse 19

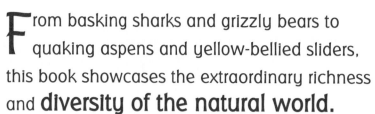

From basking sharks and grizzly bears to quaking aspens and yellow-bellied sliders, this book showcases the extraordinary richness and **diversity of the natural world.**

On a whirlwind tour through jungles, deserts, grasslands, gardens, oceans, farms and fields, you'll encounter **exactly 1000** amazing things found in nature.

The pictures are **not drawn to scale**. In real life, the tiny termite on page 8 is smaller than your fingernail, and the gigantic whale shark on page 19 is the length of a large bus.

Every picture is labelled with its name, and there is a list of all the names from aardwolf to zebra at the back of the book.